Very Rare
GLASSWARE
of the Depression Years
Third Series

Gene Florence

COLLECTOR BOOKS
A Division of Schroeder Publishing Co., Inc.

The current values in this book should be used only as a guide. They are not intended to set prices, which vary from one section of the country to another. Auction prices as well as dealer prices vary greatly and are affected by condition as well as demand. Neither the Author nor the Publisher assumes responsibility for any losses that might be incurred as a result of consulting this guide.

Searching For A Publisher?

We are always looking for knowledgeable people considered to be experts within their fields. If you feel that there is a real need for a book on your collectible subject and have a large comprehensive collection, contact us.

COLLECTOR BOOKS
P.O. Box 3009
Paducah, Kentucky 42002-3009

Other Books by Gene Florence

Collectible Glassware from the 40's, 50's, 60's $19.95
Elegant Glassware of the Depression Era, Revised 5th Edition $19.95
Kitchen Glassware of the Depression Years, 4th Edition $19.95
Pocket Guide to Depression Glass, 8th Edition $9.95
Collector's Encyclopedia of Depression Glass, 10th Edition $19.95
Collector's Encyclopedia of Occupied Japan I $14.95
Collector's Encyclopedia of Occupied Japan II $14.95
Collector's Encyclopedia of Occupied Japan III $14.95
Collector's Encyclopedia of Occupied Japan IV $14.95
Collector's Encyclopedia of Occupied Japan V $14.95
Very Rare Glassware of the Depression Years..$24.95
Very Rare Glassware of the Depression Years, 2nd Series $24.95
Gene Florence's Standard Baseball Card Guide Price Guide, 5th Edition............................$9.95
Collector's Encyclopedia of Akro Agate, Revised Edition..$14.95

Table of Contents

Foreword

The acceptance of my two earlier editions of *Very Rare Glassware of the Depression Years* has been overwhelming. I had little idea how collectors would respond to a "picture" book of rarely found items. The first book has already been reprinted twice and one of the limited (500) leather bound copies recently sold for $125. There was no limited edition of the second book and for all of you who wrote wondering why, I can only say it was a publisher's decision in order to make the first book special. As an author who loves his work, I thank you, my readers, for all the wonderful letters and phone calls asking when another *Very Rare Glassware of the Depression Years* would be available.

As with the second book, this one was easier to do than the others in many ways. Establishing a successful format is the most difficult part of any new book, and since that was already done, all I had to do was find enough rare items for another book! Once again, I am only showing rare pieces that encompass the time period and patterns shown in my other Depression Era books. I have added a couple of rarely found items from my newly released book *Collectible Glassware from the 40's, 50's, 60's*.

Finding the glassware was easier this time since many collectors sought me out to advise me of their treasures after seeing the earlier books. Several pieces that were to be included will have to wait until next time since deadlines arrived before I could obtain the pictures. Several collectors found that photography of glassware is not an easy task and are going to lend me the glass for my photographer to try and capture their prized possessions. That makes a fast start for the next book. Without you keeping watch for unknown glassware pieces, I could never have found enough pieces to put this book together in the two years that it took.

Again photographs for this book were taken over a two year period. After newly discovered items or unusual colors of commonly found pieces were discovered, I had them photographed at the earliest opportunity. This sounds simple enough, but when you are dealing with a commercial photographer with thousands of prints and a publisher with hundreds of books in the works, even after shots are taken photographs sometimes end up missing! Too, it is difficult to get some pieces to show both color and pattern, but finally getting it photographed, even if it took two or three photography sessions to do it, never seemed to solve the problem of where the print was when you needed it! Adding to that problem is my working out of my Florida home now. Instead of driving 260 miles from Lexington to Paducah, I have to go from Florida to Lexington and then to Paducah. That adds over 800 miles to get photographs; so I have to plan even more efficiently.

Rare glass continues to be found! The last photograph shown in this book turned up too late to include in its rightful place under Jeannette, but it was too valuable a find to leave out! Unbelievably, so many readers found the heretofore elusive Heisey Crystolite cake stands after it was shown in the first book that it is no longer considered rare! After the second book, Heisey Plantation 5" epergne candle holders and Imperial pink Beaded Block pitchers seemed to be found in quantities. What will it be this time? These items are still avidly sought, however. Glass enthusiasts hope that will happen to some of the items shown in this book!

Hopefully, you will appreciate our efforts in putting this third book on rare Depression Era glassware together. I hope it helps you find some rare glass! Let me know; maybe you will find some pieces we can use in the next book!

Acknowledgments

Many collectors have loaned their rare glass for photographs in this book, and each is acknowledged with the items shown. However, many collectors went beyond lending glass to be shown. A special thanks to Dick and Pat Spencer who brought not only their glass, but the glass of several other collectors from Illinois and Missouri. (Dick has recently found out that writing is even more fun than photo sessions with his work on a soon to be released book on glass animals!) Bill and Lottie Porter, with grandson Quinten Keech, came from Michigan with Lottie's glass. Lottie had just gotten out of the hospital two days before she came to Paducah; that is how important letting collectors see rare glass is to her! All of these fine folks helped unpack and repack their prized glassware for photography so that you could see the rarest Depression Era glassware that can be found. If it were not for these special people who are willing to share their collections with others, a book of this magnitude would be nearly impossible to do.

Photography for this book was done by Tom Clouser of Curtis and Mays Studio in Paducah, Kentucky. Assisting in layouts at the photography sessions from Collector Books were Jane White, Gail Ashburn, and Lisa Stroup. Photographs of the "Experimental Blue" Heisey were taken by Kenn Whitmyer.

Family has always been important to me in my work. Mom, "Grannie Bear," lists and packs glass while Dad washes it for all the photography sessions with my sons, Chad and Marc, helping me load and unload glass for each session. Cathy, my wife, continues to be my proofreader and general taskmaster. She attempts to put my varied ideas in a comprehensible form for the public. She and her mother, Sibyl, take two weeks, five tables and three rooms of the house to do most of the packing and correlating of patterns of glass for the photography sessions. Even with all this help, the many tasks needed to accomplish this work are beginning to need more hands. Please know how very much we appreciate readers' and collectors' input of glass and information.

Many people work behind the scenes to put a book together. Much praise belongs to unseen workers who make this book into a usable format. Layout is vital. It is important to get picture and type sizes to fit and all horizontal photos and verticals to blend; and placing patterns alphabetically by company does create a layout problem or two! Sherry Kraus of Collector Books is responsible for the meshing of this into a workable format. Cathy, Grannie Bear and I proofed and corrected along with Collector Books' staff. All headaches and other problems with photographs disappearing and deadlines being met were given to the new editor, Lisa Stroup. If I've overlooked someone, forgive me; it was not intentional. Please know I'm thankful for all your efforts. I could not have finished this book without your efforts!

CAMBRIDGE GLASS COMPANY 1902 – 1958

The Cambridge Glass Company was started in Cambridge, Ohio, in 1902. Glass was made there until 1958, except for a short period in 1954 – 1955 when the plant was closed. Today, there is a National Cambridge Collector's Club. A Cambridge Museum is operated by that club and located on Rt. 40E in Cambridge, Ohio.

The glass photographed in this section represents the patterns made during the 1930's to the 1950's that are most collected today. Collectors of Cambridge glass began collecting the glass by colors and decorations that were distinctly Cambridge. However, as more and more Depression glass collectors started to notice the finer handmade glassware from Cambridge, dinnerware lines and sets began to be gathered. Thus, a new standard of collecting was created and the prices started rising.

If you are interested in joining the National Cambridge Collectors Club, their address is:

National Cambridge Collectors, Inc.,
P.O. Box 416GF,
Cambridge, Ohio 43725

Dues are $15.00 a year.

The following pages show some of the rarest pieces of Cambridge known in the dinnerware lines with emphasis on color rarities as well as unusual pieces.

From the collection of Dennis Bialek

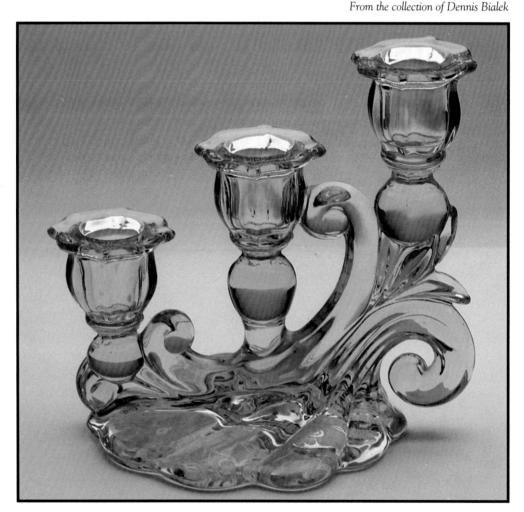

APPLE BLOSSOM *blue candlestick – rare item*
This Moonlight Blue Caprice #1338 6″ 3-lite candlestick is etched with Apple Blossom design.

CAPRICE *amber water goblet – rare color*
This goblet was purchased at the Peach State Depression Glass Show
in Marietta, Georgia, a few years ago.

CAPRICE *Moonlight Blue Doulton style 90 oz. pitcher – rare item*

CAPRICE *crystal pressed unknown stemware line sherbet – rare item*

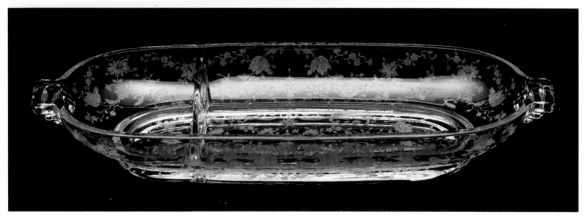

CHANTILLY *crystal two part divided relish – unusual item*

CHANTILLY *crystal Pristine 225 9″ blown divided bowl – rare item*

CHANTILLY *crystal Pristine 485 9½″ crescent salad plate – rare item*

Author's Collection

CLEO *amber #94 vase (7" x 8¼") – rare item*

Author's Collection

CLEO *Willow Blue #638 triple candleholder – rare item*

From the collection of Dennis Bialek

CLEO *green 12 oz. tumbler – rare item*

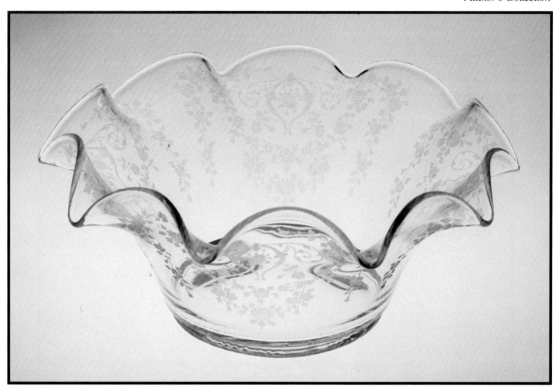

DIANE *crystal 10" ruffled bowl – unusual mould*

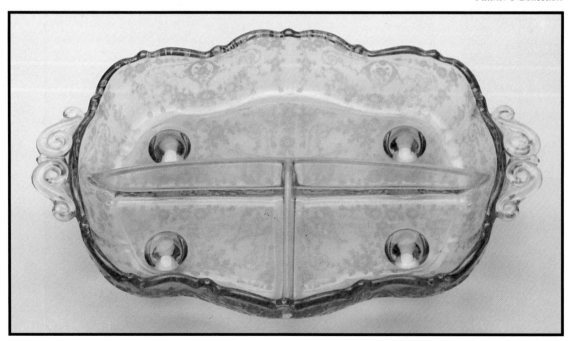

DIANE *iridized #3900/126 12", 3 part relish and celery – rare color*
Rarely are Cambridge items found onto which the pattern was etched after the iridized spray was applied. Usually this was done outside the factory after the piece was etched; that this was factory applied is the unusual part.

DIANE *Emerald Green #968 sea food cocktail – rare color*

DIANE *crystal #3400/161, 6 oz. footed oil – rare item*

Author's Collection

DIANE *crystal #3400/92 2½ oz. tumbler and #3400/118 35 oz. decanter – rare items*

ELAINE *crystal #1701, 9″ top hat vase – rare item*

From the collection of Dick and Pat Spencer

ELAINE *crystal 3500/109 11", 4 toed oval ram's head bowl – rare item*
Bowl is shown from different angles to display ram's head.

GLORIA *amber #1070 2 oz. pinch tumbler and #1070 36 oz. pinch decanter – rare color*

GLORIA
Ebony with silver decoration #646
5" candleholder – rare color

GLORIA *Ebony with silver decoration #3400/4, 12", 4 toed bowl – rare color*

GLORIA *Heatherbloom #3035 1 oz. cordial – rare color*

Author's Collection

GLORIA *Gold Krystol #8161 2 oz. tumbler and #3400/92 32 oz. ball shape decanter – rare color*

IMPERIAL HUNT SCENE *amber, gold encrusted #3075/6 80 oz. covered jug – rare color*

Author's Collection

PORTIA *amber #3400/113 handled decanter – rare color and item*

PORTIA *crystal with gold decoration #3400/69 after dinner cup and saucer – rare item*

PORTIA *crystal #3500/78 6" ram's head candy box and cover – rare item*

Author's Collection

ROSALIE *(#731) Bluebell #3077 9 oz. water goblet – rare color*

ROSALIE *(#731) Topaz #3123 Aero Optic 8 oz. water – rare color*

ROSALIE (#731) *Willow Blue #1070*
2 oz. tumbler – rare color

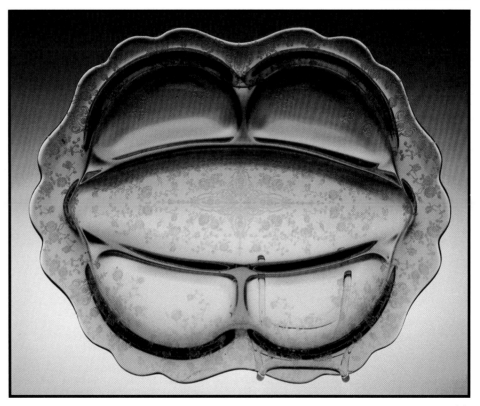

ROSEPOINT *amber #3400/67 12″, 5 compartment celery and relish – rare color*

ROSEPOINT *crystal Pristine 18″ pan bowl – rare item*
Evidently this bowl was difficult to make since the bottom is curved upward instead of being flat.

ROSEPOINT *crystal #944 sugar and creamer – rare items*

Author's Collection

ROSEPOINT *crystal #3400/201*
4 toed bonbon – rare item
Views from each end are shown.

ROSEPOINT *crystal Pristine #500, 6½″ (Leaf) candlestick – rare item*

Author's Collection

ROSEPOINT *crystal Pristine #419, 12" 6 part relish – rare item*

ROSEPOINT *crystal Pristine #572 6" vase – rare item*

From the collection of Sam and Becky Collings

ROSEPOINT *Ebony, gold encrusted, #300 7", 3 footed candy – rare color*

From the collection of Sam and Becky Collings

ROSEPOINT *Ebony, gold encrusted #278 11″ vase – rare color*

SQUARE *crystal tumbler with*
"crackle" effect – rare item

SQUARE *crystal tumbler*
with ruffled top to make vase – rare item

WILDFLOWER *Emerald #1238 12" vase – rare color*

Author's Collection

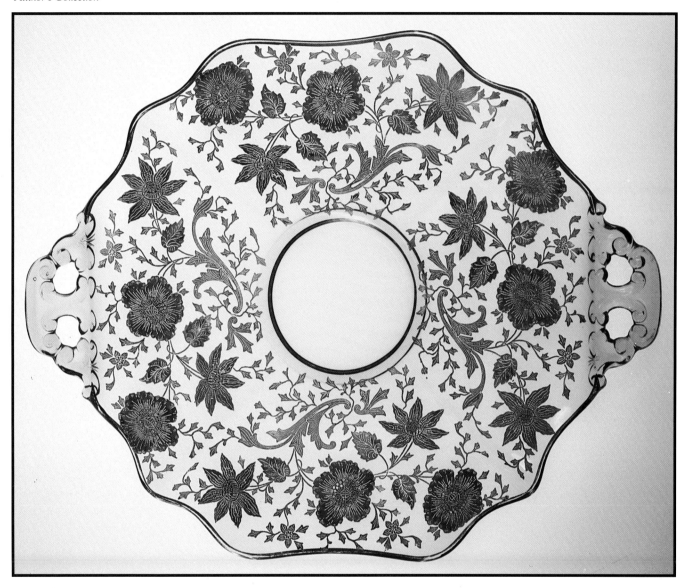

WILDFLOWER *amber, gold encrusted #3400/35 11", 2 handled plate – rare color*

DUNCAN & MILLER GLASS COMPANY 1893 – 1955

The new Duncan & Miller Glass Company was incorporated in 1900 after beginning as the Duncan Glass Company in Pittsburgh and moving to Washington, Pennsylvania, in 1893. Although Duncan's glassware was not as widely distributed as some of the other glass companies', there are many collectors seeking it today.

The patterns made during and shortly after the Depression years are in demand with collectors. One of the more popular patterns with collectors is the Caribbean pattern made from 1936 until 1955. Although blue Caribbean is the most sought color, there are also those seeking the crystal.

Author's Collection

CARIBBEAN *blue opalescent 9" salad bowl – rare color*

FEDERAL GLASS COMPANY 1900 – 1984

Federal Glass company was founded in Columbus, Ohio, and really prospered during the Depression with its dinnerware sets in pink, blue, green, and the prolific amber known as "Golden Glo" used in the patterns of Madrid, Patrician, Sharon and Parrot.

Federal became the first major company to reproduce a pattern from the Depression era with each piece marked. "Recollection" was patterned from the original Madrid, issued in 1976 for the bicentennial and marked with '76 on each piece. These moulds were later sold to Indiana Glass Company and the '76 removed. Today, Indiana still makes the Madrid pattern in several colors and pieces that were not originally made.

Author's Collection

MADRID *Golden Glo ash tray – rare item*
In the early 1970's I bought a large set of amber Madrid just to get an ash tray!
At that time no one had ever seen one!

GEORGIAN *green lazy susan or cold cuts server – rare item*
I have only seen two of these in all my travels. It is the same walnut base that is used for the Madrid set which was shown in the second edition of this book. To my knowledge there have not been any of the indented coasters found in Georgian. As on the tumblers and some of the dinners, there are no "lovebirds" on these pieces.

From the collection of Dan Tucker and Lorrie Kitchen

PARROT *Golden Glo paperweight – rare item*
When moulds were cold, a piece of glass was used to "warm-in" the mould
and this may have been such an item.

FENTON ART GLASS COMPANY 1907 *to Date*

The first glassware was made at this plant in 1907 and it is still being made at the original site in Williamstown, West Virginia. Fenton made more Carnival and Art glass than they did glassware that is considered Depression ware. Lincoln Inn was one of their major patterns of this time period, and the multitude of colors introduced in that line is astonishing. Begun in 1928, Lincoln Inn was made as late as the 1980's in an iridescent purple color.

Fenton Art Glass is still one of the few major glass companies that is continuing to operate in today's economy! Many gift shops and country stores carry Fenton's line and their adaptability to meet the public's demand for gift glassware has allowed them to continue to prosper in this changing world.

Author's Collection

LINCOLN INN *opalescent green sugar bowl – rare color*

FOSTORIA GLASS COMPANY 1887 – 1986

Fostoria Glass Company almost survived a century! That included a major move from Fostoria, Ohio, to Moundsville, West Virginia, in the early days. Lancaster Colony bought Fostoria in the early 1980's but the glassware in the morgue at the factory was sold as late as December 1986.

The American pattern, first begun in1915, was one of the longest made patterns in U.S. glass-making history! Lancaster Colony is continuing to make pieces available in this pattern through Indiana Glass Company and Dalzell Viking Glass Company.

From the collection of Kenn and Margaret Whitmyer

AMERICAN *opaque blue 3″ hat – rare color*

AMERICAN *blue 5¾", 6 oz. cologne bottle – rare color*

AMERICAN *crystal Tom & Jerry punch bowl – rare style*
Another bowl in green and the one shown in blue in the second edition are the only other bowls found in this style.
Since these were found in green and blue, it stands to reason that they were made very early in this line.
This crystal bowl was in a furniture container shipped back from England, as so many of the rarely found American
pieces have been! Yes, Fostoria's American was marketed in England.

"AMERICAN LADY" *amethyst with silver coating 4", 3½" cocktail – rare item*
The #2056½ American line has been dubbed "American Lady" by collectors.

Author's Collection

"AMERICAN LADY" *green with silver coating 4", 3½" cocktail – rare item*

Author's Collection

COLONY *opaque blue 5 ¼", 9 oz. water goblet – rare color*

From the collection of Bill and Barbara Adt

NAVARRE *crystal 32 oz. carafe – rare item*

HAZEL-ATLAS GLASS COMPANY 1902 – 1956

Hazel-Atlas was formed from the merger of Hazel Glass Company and Atlas Glass and Metal Company in 1902. Production of containers and tumblers were their main concern until the Depression years. In the 1930's, starting with kitchenware items such as colored mixing bowls, they quickly branched into dinnerware patterns.

The Shirley Temple bowl, mug and creamer that are recognized by almost everyone were made by Hazel-Atlas. Sets of Royal Lace and Moderntone in Ritz blue (cobalt) were advertised together for the same price: 44 pieces for $2.99!

Now, there is a much greater price range in those patterns!

In recent years, it has been the kitchenware made by Hazel-Atlas that has come to the forefront. Again, the popularity of Ritz blue has pushed the prices of that color well above the prices for pink and green. Mixing bowls, measuring cups, and creamers all command premium prices. The piece may be rarer in some other color, but collector demand pushes the price of the blue well beyond those of any other color.

Author's Collection

OVIDE "ART DECO" *decorated sugar bowl – rare decoration*

52

OVIDE "ART DECO" *decorated creamer – rare decoration*
In twenty years of searching this creamer and sugar are the only two pieces of this decorated
Ovide I have been able to purchase.

A.H. HEISEY & COMPANY 1896 – 1957

A.H. Heisey & Company opened its door in 1896. Their handsome pressed glassware was a success. In fact, the innovative idea of advertising glassware in national publications is attributed to Heisey. Glass was made continuously at the plant site in Newark, Ohio, until 1957. As with Cambridge, the glassware made in the 1930's to 1950's is the most collectible today.

One of the most difficult problems facing new collectors comes from the fact that the Heisey moulds were bought by Imperial in 1958, and many pieces were made at that plant until its demise in 1984. New collectors have to learn the Imperial colors because some of these pieces made by Imperial are similar to rare Heisey colors. Crystal pieces are more difficult to distinguish and collectors are beginning to accept this fact. Almost all of those Heisey/Imperial moulds were repurchased by the Heisey Collectors of America, Inc. and are now back in Newark, Ohio. So, there should be no danger of reissues being made from these moulds again.

From the collection of Dick and Pat Spencer

EMPRESS *or* QUEEN ANNE #1509 *crystal 3 footed 3″ individual candlestick – rare item*
*Most crystal Empress is considered to be Queen Anne. The names refer to different **time periods only** since the patterns are the same.*

From the collection of Gary and Sue Clark

EMPRESS *#1401 Moongleam 6″ compotier, dolphin footed – rare item*

From the collection of Gary and Sue Clark

EMPRESS #1401 Moongleam 16″ four part buffet relish – rare item

EMPRESS *#1401 Moongleam tumbler, 8 oz., dolphin footed – rare item*

LODESTAR *handled sugar bowl – rare item*

RIBBON OCTAGON *#1231 cobalt rum pot – rare item and color*

Author's Collection

RIBBON OCTAGON *#1231 crystal rum pot – rare item*

Author's Collection

RIBBON OCTAGON *#1231 Sahara rum pot – rare item and color*
These rum pots can be found with or without a glass stopper. Those
which have stoppers have ground spouts to make the stopper fit properly.

From the collection of Dick and Pat Spencer

MEASURE CUP *crystal – rare item*

Author's Collection

ORCHID *crystal finger bowl – rare item*
This finger bowl is heavier and an entirely different mould than those that are usually seen.

Author's Collection

ORCHID URN *#5012 crystal 12″ square*
footed bud vase – rare item

Author's Collection

ORCHID URN #5012 crystal 9″ footed vase – rare item

Author's Collection

PLANTATION *crystal 9″, footed, flared vase – rare item*

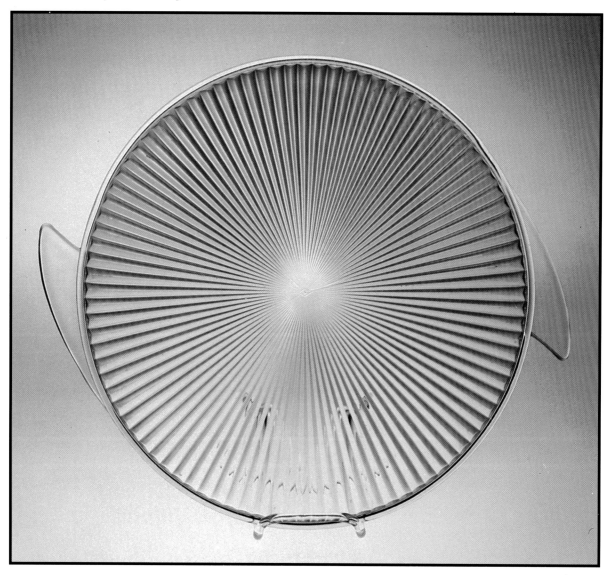

RIDGELEIGH *#1469 12″ handled crystal cake plate – rare item*

From the collection of Dick and Pat Spencer

SATURN *zircon cup and saucer – rare color*

From the collection of Dick and Pat Spencer

SATURN *zircon 10¾" bowl – rare color*

WAVERLY *crystal lion cover trinket box – rare item*
After Imperial reproduced these in amber the price of the crystal took a nose dive and has never fully recovered!

WAVERLY #1519 4½"crystal candlestick – rare item

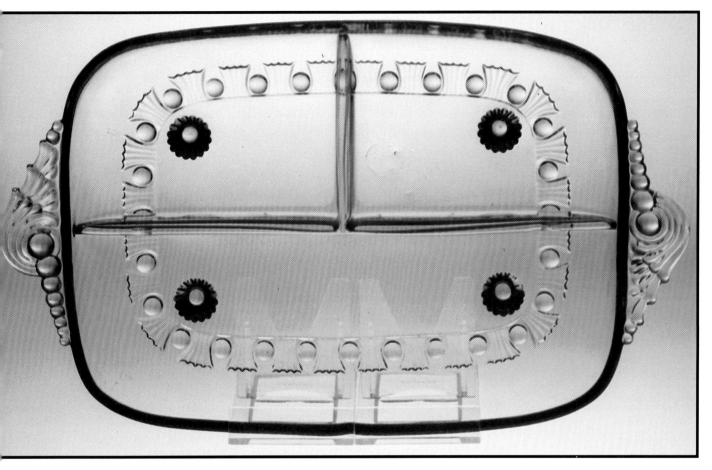

ZIRCON #1495 FERN *pattern divided relish – rare color*

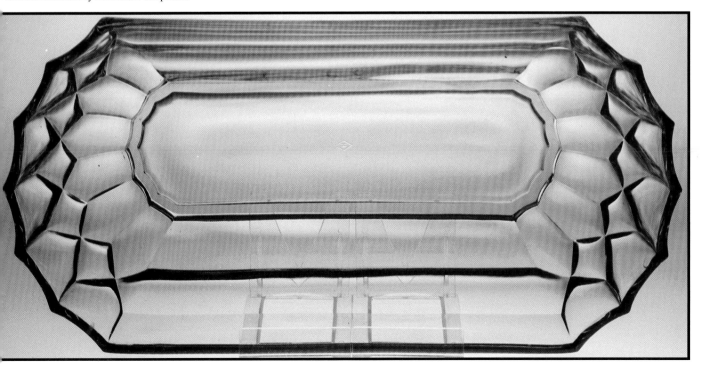

ZIRCON #1488 KOHINOOR *pattern 14" floral bowl – rare color*

**EXPERIMENTAL BLUE
ALBEMARLE** *pattern*
5 oz. sherbets – rare color
*Note that the top sherbet has a crystal
stem with a blue optic top while the
bottom sherbet is all blue with no optic.
The optic makes the blue seem more
pronounced.*

Both sherbets from the collection of Jim and Helen Kennon

EXPERIMENTAL BLUE ALBEMARLE *pattern 5 oz. footed sodas – rare color
Note the top soda has a blue top and foot with a crystal stem while the middle one has a blue
top and crystal stem and foot. The bottom soda is all blue. These were really experimental!*

HOCKING GLASS COMPANY 1905 *to Date*

Hocking became today's Anchor-Hocking in 1937, but nearly all of the glassware shown in this section was made before the year of the merger. The people who work at this factory have always helped me in every way they could in my research because they realize the historical significance of our glass. I am truly grateful.

Author's Collection

BUBBLE *Sapphire blue 9" flanged bowl – rare item*
I have only heard of three of these now in collections.

Author's Collection

BLOCK OPTIC *pink 3½" wine goblet – rare item*
Although a dozen of this size goblet in green Cameo have surfaced over the years, this pink one is the only Block Optic 3½" short wine to have been uncovered at this time.

COLONIAL *white 5", 16 oz. creamer – rare color*

COLONIAL
white sugar bowl – rare color
This set was found in Washington Court House, Ohio, a few years ago. No lid has been seen, but I would not rule out its existence.

Author's Collection

"LACE EDGE," OLD COLONY
crystal cookie jar – rare color
How many crystal cookie jars
have you seen?

Author's Collection

"LACE EDGE," OLD COLONY *green 6⅜" cereal bowl – rare color*
Most pieces found in green Old Colony turn out to be made by some company other than
Hocking, but this **is** *Hocking!*

From the collection of Earl and Beverly Hines

MAYFAIR *green 3¾", 1 oz. cordial – rare item*

MAYFAIR *pink round cup – rare item*
There are two different moulds for this cup. The thin style is shown, but there is also a thicker
style. This is doubly unusual in that there were two separate moulds
for such a rarely seen item.

From the collection of Kenn and Margaret Whitmyer

MISS AMERICA *pink comport – rare item*
The normally found 5" comport was flattened after being made!

MISS AMERICA blue 3⁷⁄₁₆″ sherbet – rare color

MISS AMERICA
Royal Ruby 3⁷⁄₁₆″ sherbet – rare color

MISS AMERICA
Royal Ruby 3⁵⁄₁₆″ sherbet – rare color

Note that the top and middle sherbet are "flared" out while the bottom sherbet is not. The sherbet in the middle is very amberina in color.

MISS AMERICA *Royal Ruby creamer – rare color*
Very few pieces of Royal Ruby Miss America have ever been found, but all
the pieces shown here were part of a Hocking retiree's
grandson's fifty piece collection.

Author's Collection

MISS AMERICA *Royal Ruby sugar – rare color*

MISS AMERICA *Royal Ruby 5⅜″, 8 oz. water goblet – rare color*

Author's Collection

MISS AMERICA *Royal Ruby 5 ⁷⁄₁₆″, 8¾ oz. water goblet – rare color*
Notice how the top of this water goblet "flares out"
while the one on page 82 does not.

MISS AMERICA *Royal Ruby 4", 5 oz. juice tumbler – rare color*
One of the unusual things about this set of Miss America is that most of
the pieces have ground bottoms typical of hand made, more
expensively manufactured, glassware.

From the collection of Bill and Lottie Porter

PRINCESS *blue cup and saucer – rare color*

IMPERIAL GLASS CORPORATION 1904 – 1984

Although glass making began at Imperial in 1904, it was the start of a new era in 1936 when Candlewick was introduced for the first time. Until the company's demise in 1984, Imperial turned out a multitude of pieces in this pattern; but it was not their only pattern.

Author's Collection

CANDLEWICK *Viennese blue #400/37 cup and saucer – rare color*

CANDLEWICK *black 8″, 4 toed #400/74B round bowl – rare color*

Author's Collection

CANDLEWICK *yellow #400/133 5" ash tray – rare item*
This ash tray was made during WWII and displays the stars and stripes on a shield.

CANDLEWICK *crystal #400/125A 11" divided oval bowl – rare item*
Both a side and end view are shown so you can see the scalloped partition.

From the collection of Dick and Pat Spencer

CANDLEWICK *crystal #400/224 5½" candlestick – rare item*

CANDLEWICK *crystal #400/137 footed oval compote – rare item*

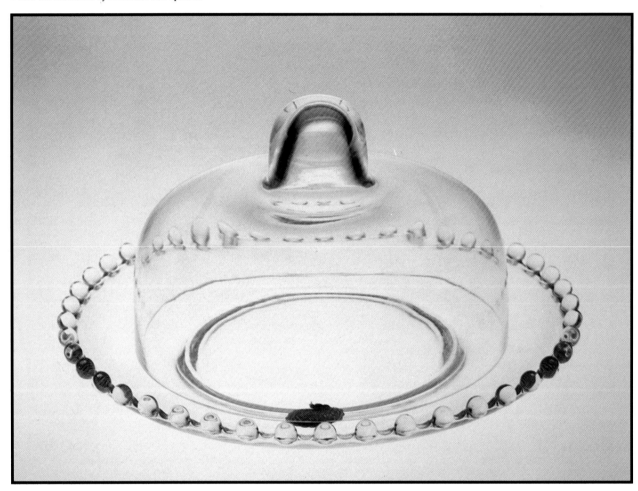

CANDLEWICK *crystal #400/123 toast and cover – rare item*

CANDLEWICK *crystal #400/29 7" tray – rare item*
This tray has an Orchid etching and was probably meant to
have sterling silver applied.

From the collection of Dick and Pat Spencer

CANDLEWICK *charcoal #400/655 jar tower – rare item*
Many collectors do not recognize this as a Candlewick piece.

CAPE COD *crystal #160/90 4" Aladdin style candle holder – rare item*
This was only made in 1951 so there are not many of these found in collections.

INDIANA GLASS COMPANY 1907 *to Date*

Indiana Glass has caused concern for collector's for years with their "re-issues." A more proper term might be reproductions! It is a shame because many pieces of their glass fit the "rare" category.

From the collection of Dan Tucker and Lorrie Kitchen

NO. 612 *green butter top paperweight – rare item*
Many slabs of glass were made by workers when a mould was first heated (warmed in) and that was probably the reason that items such as this are occasionally found today.

NO. 612 "HORSESHOE"
green 4¼", 9 oz. flat tumbler – rare item
The first one of these to be found was in 1971 at the
Washington Court House, Ohio, flea market. I paid
$1.00 for it and later sold it for $5.00, a tidy profit for
a schoolteacher in those days.

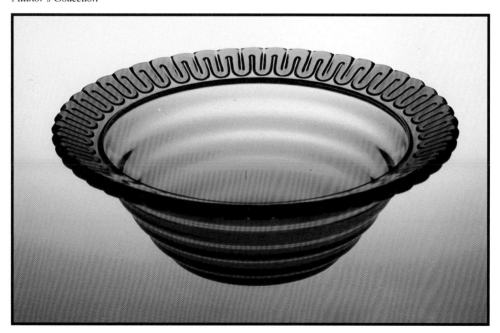

NO. 624 "CHRISTMAS CANDY" *Terrace Green 9½" bowl – rare item*

JEANETTE GLASS COMPANY

Jeannette Glass Company seemed to have an affinity for making odd-colored glass from their standard glassware lines. Canary yellow (vaseline), red or even Delphite blue turns up in patterns once in a while. What makes this fact even more astounding is that those colors were not part of their repertoire in other patterns either. It's as if they wanted to cause us wonderment years later.

From the collection of Bill and Lottie Porter

ADAM *yellow cup with round saucer — rare color and shape*
In early 1973 seven of these sets were found and this is one of those sets.
Only round saucers have been seen in yellow — never in the normally found squared shape!

From the collection of Bill and Lottie Porter

CHERRY BLOSSOM *amber child's cup and saucer – rare color*

From the collection of Parke and Joyce Bloyer

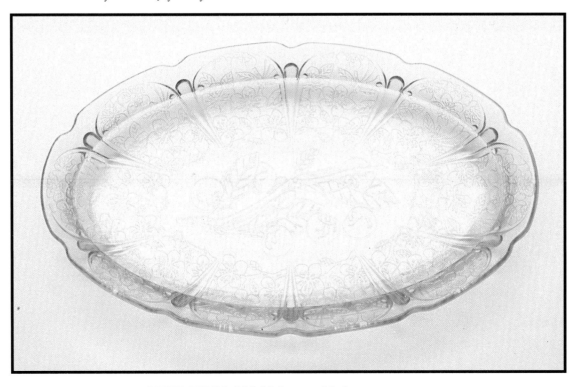

CHERRY BLOSSOM *green 9" platter – rare item*

Author's collection

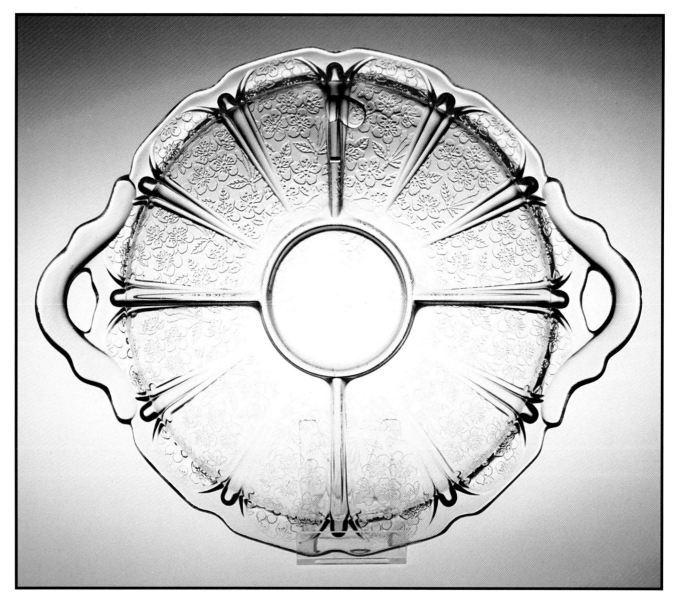

CHERRY BLOSSOM *pink five part 10½" relish tray – rare item*
Only two of these have been seen. This one has a large bubble in the glass and the other one also had a large bubble, but it was on the edge and has broken out. Evidently, these relish trays caused problems in manufacturing and were not added to the array of Cherry Blossom items.

From the collection of Bill and Lottie Porter

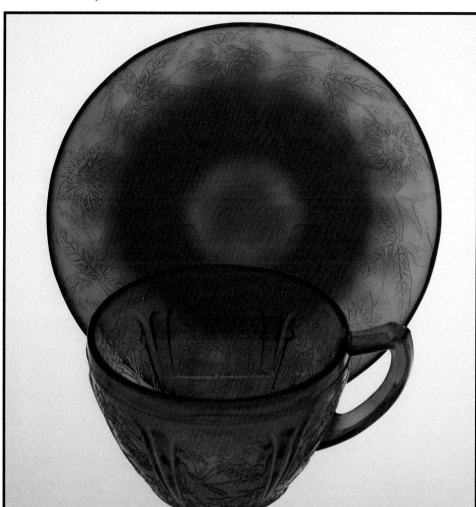

CHERRY BLOSSOM *red cup/***FLORAL** *red saucer – rare color*
Although the Cherry Blossom cups have been reproduced in red, notice the three concentric
rings near the top edge of this old cup. The new ones do not have these bands.

Author's Collection

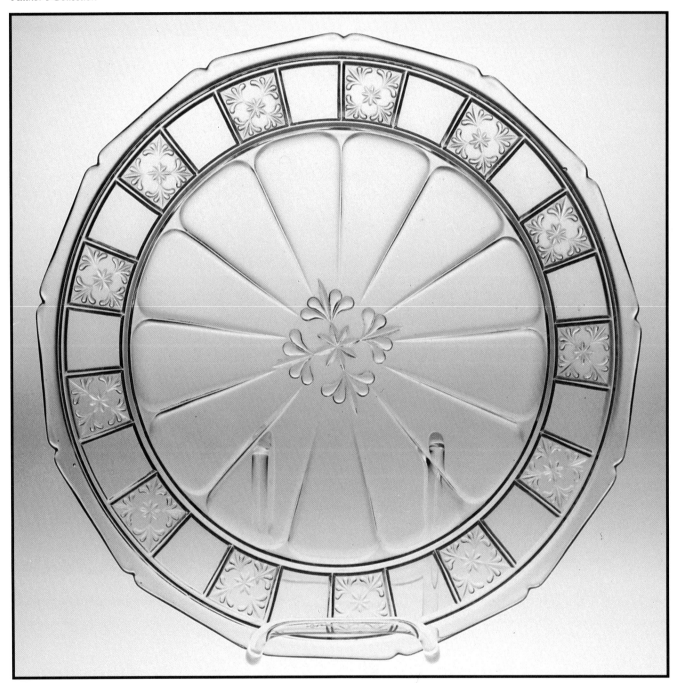

DORIC *pink 9" serrated plate – rare item*
This plate was purchased in the early 1970's and only one other has surfaced in all these years.

From the collection of Earl and Beverly Hines

FLORAL *crystal three legged flared rose bowl w/flower frog – rare item*
A few of these bowls have been found in crystal and green, but only three or four of the
frogs have been found.

FLORAL *Delphite blue platter – rare color*
You have to turn over the platter in order to see the complete pattern,
so I have given you both views.

From the collection of Earl and Beverly Hines

FLORAL *green three legged rose bowl – rare item*

From the collection of Earl and Beverly Hines

FLORAL *pink ice tub – rare item*
This ice tub was found in an antique mall in Indiana in 1981 and was the last of the six known to be found.

Author's Collection

FRUITS *green 5", 12 oz. ice tea tumbler – rare item*
Note the cluster of cherries hanging from leaves, as opposed to Cherry Blossom which has blossoms.

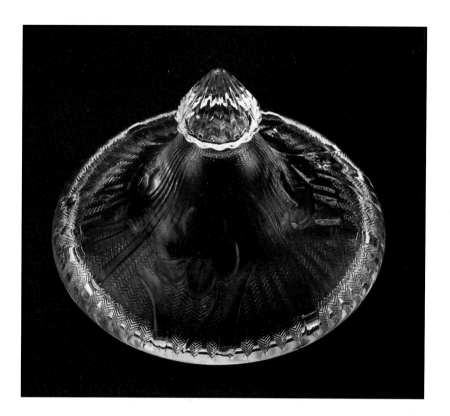

IRIS *crystal sugar lid – rare style
This sugar lid is less domed than the
normally seen lid. It is shown
separately and on the sugar.*

From the collection of Dan Kramer

Author's Collection

IRIS *pink 9" vase – rare color*
Most pink vases found are very light in color, but this one is very vivid.

SHELL PINK

Opaque pink 9" heavy bottom vase – rare item
Since I put this pattern in my new book, Collectible
Glassware from the 40's, 50's, 60's... there has been a
rush to find these Shell Pink items; both items pictured here
are causing collectors' headaches.

Author's Collection

Author's Collec

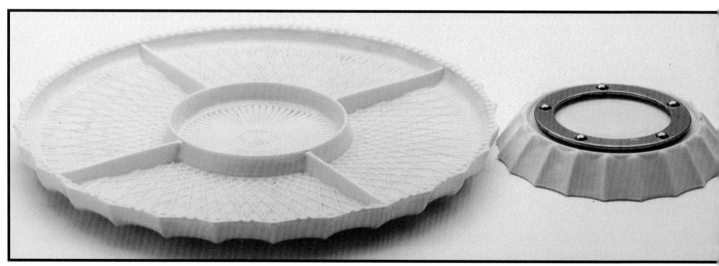

SHELL PINK *opaque pink lazy susan – rare item*
It is the base of this item that is hard to find; I have pictured it separately so you can tell what it looks like if you see it out by itsel

Author's Collection

SUNFLOWER *Delphite blue creamer – rare color*

SWIRL *Ultramarine 48 oz. footed pitcher – rare item*

LANCASTER GLASS COMPANY 1908 – 1937

Although purchased by Hocking in 1924, Lancaster Glass of Lancaster, Ohio, operated under that name until 1937 when Hocking eliminated the name completely. This plant still operates today as plant #2 of Anchor-Hocking.

Author's collection

JUBILEE *yellow 11" center handle server – rare item*

MACBETH-EVANS GLASS COMPANY 1899 – 1937

Macbeth-Evans made some of the more popular Depression patterns, but as in other companies' wares, some pieces are in such short supply, they're deemed quite rare finds.

From the collection of Bill and Lottie Porter

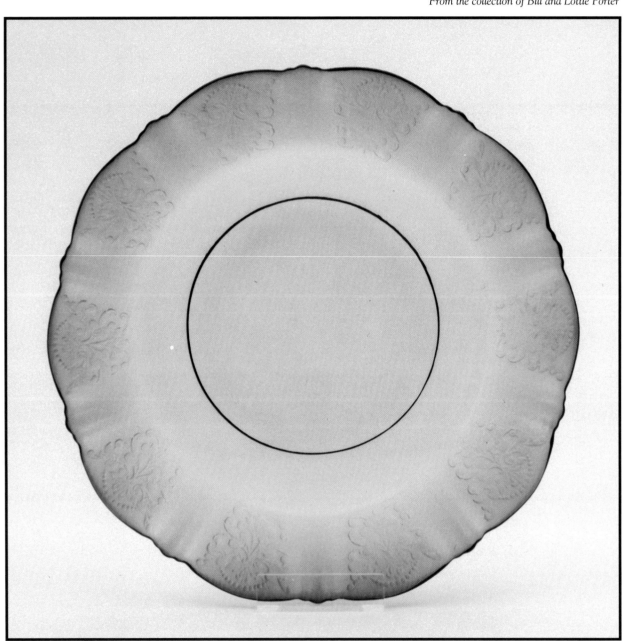

AMERICAN SWEETHEART *Smoke 9½" flat soup – rare color*

McKEE GLASS COMPANY 1853 – 1951

The company was originally founded as McKee & Brothers Glass Works at Pittsburgh in Westmoreland County in 1888 and built its new plant there. This site became the town of Jeannette. The move had been necessitated by the availability of natural gas in this area. Later, with the depletion of this natural gas, the company turned to the other readily available fuel in the area – coal. McKee continued making glass at this site until 1951 when the Thatcher Glass Company bought the company.

When McKee is mentioned today, two things seem to stand out in collector's minds: Rock Crystal and kitchenware items. Collectors of Depression patterns immediately think of the red or crystal Rock Crystal pattern that was made from the early 1900's until the 1940's. Kitchenware lines of reamers and measuring cups have come to the forefront of collecting in recent years. Many other kitchenware items were made, but these two categories include some of the most avidly sought items. Below is a rare candlestick from one of the few patterns made from their Jade Green kitchenware color.

Author's Collection

LAUREL *Jade Green three footed candlestick – rare item*

ROCK CRYSTAL *green fancy tankard pitcher – rare item*

From the collection of Cathy Florence

ROCK CRYSTAL *red lamp – rare item*

Author's Collection

ROCK CRYSTAL *orange slag 12½″ footed center bowl – rare color*
Bowl is shown from two views in order to show the pattern.

Author's Collection

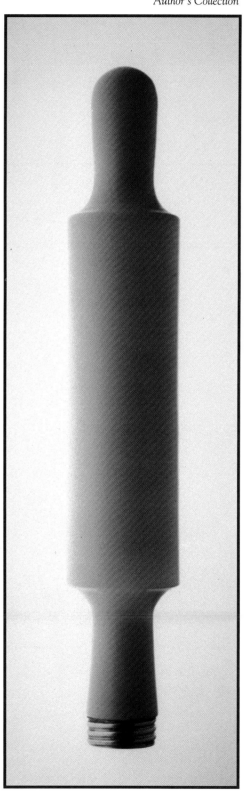

ROLLING PIN *Chalaine Blue – rare color*
This rolling pin has been in our collection since 1982, but there are several collectors trying to pry it loose.

MORGANTOWN GLASS WORKS 1929 – 1972

First established in Morgantown, West Virginia, as Morgantown Glass Works, it became the Economy Glass Tumbler Co. in the early 1900's and stayed thus until 1929 when it became Morgantown again. It was continued as Morgantown until bought out by Bailey Glass in 1972.

Author's Collection

SUNRISE MEDALLION "DANCING GIRL" *green sugar bowl – rare item*

NEW MARTINSVILLE GLASS MANUFACTURING COMPANY 1901 – 1944

The factory became Viking Glass Company in 1944 and is still in operation today. Although they produced a multitude of colors during the Depression era, New Martinsville exhibited quality color control and were known for their Ruby (red) and their Ritz blue (cobalt blue).

RADIANCE *pink cup and saucer – rare color*

MOONDROPS *Ritz blue 4¾" "rocket" wine and "rocket" decanter – rare items*

MOONDROPS *dark green "rocket" bud vase – rare item*

MOONDROPS *ruby 4⅞" 9 oz. tumbler w/sterling silver decoration – rare decoration*

PADEN CITY GLASS COMPANY 1916 – 1951

Paden City Glass Company built its factory and started producing glassware all within a one-year time period. That was considered quite a feat in 1916. We think of Paden City as a company which produced a multitude of colors and made a variety of patterns containing birds. This handmade glass was not turned out in the large quantities that many of the glass factories of that day produced. Hence, items manufactured by Paden City are even more scarce 50 years later. Most of the glassware made by this company is exceedingly attractive in design.

From the collection of Bill and Lottie Porter

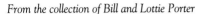

BLACK FOREST *red cup and saucer – rare item*

BLACK FOREST *pink 8½", 28 oz. decanter and 2½", 2 oz. shot glass – rare items*

BLACK FOREST *green covered 10½", 5 part relish – rare item*

Author's Collection

CUPID *pink 8¼″ elliptical vase – rare item*

CUPID *green samovar – rare item*

Author's Collection

CUPID *cobalt blue vase with silver overlay design – rare color*
This vase and the orchid colored one on the next page are stamped "Germany" on
the base. One was purchased in California at the Pasadena Junior College flea
market and the other was found in Florida at the Mt. Dora Renninger's twin
markets. The silver overlay is an exact replica of the Paden City etching. If anyone
has a idea on this, please help us solve the mystery!

Author's Collection

CUPID *orchid vase with silver overlay design – rare color*

Author's Collection

ORCHID *red footed comport – rare item*

From the collection of Bill and Lottie Porter

"NORA BIRD" *pink 4" tumbler – rare item*

"PEACOCK REVERSE" *green candy – rare item*

PYREX CORNING GLASS WORKS

Because of its longevity, Pyrex, today, is a household name. The "clambroth" white piece below is unusual since most "clambroth" pieces from this period are not marked as to origin. ("Clambroth" is a collectors' name for this translucent white color.)

"CLAMBROTH" *oval casserole – rare item*
This casserole is embossed "Pyrex" on one end and "193-197" on the other.

TIFFIN GLASS COMPANY *(one of many branches of U.S. Glass Company)*

The "R" factory of the U.S. Glass Company was located at Tiffin, Ohio. It was better known as the Tiffin Glass Factory.

Author's Collection

FUCHSIA *crystal #17457 "S" stem cordial – rare item*

FUCHSIA *crystal cocktail shaker – rare item*

U. S. GLASS COMPANY 1891 – 1962

The U. S. Glass Company was founded in 1891 as a merger of eighteen smaller companies in Ohio, Pennsylvania, and West Virginia. While Flower Garden and Butterfly remains the most popular pattern collected from U.S. Glass, "Deerwood" or "Birch Tree" is beginning to attract many admirers.

"DEERWOOD" *pink cup and saucer – rare item*

"DEERWOOD" *black handled vase – rare item*

IRIS *brown water tumbler – rare color*
Two of these tumblers were purchased in a Daytona flea market about ten years ago. I purchased one of these after this book was already laid out, but this unusual piece of Iris had to be included!

PRICE GUIDE

Page 6
APPLE BLOSSOM blue candlestick – $250.00-300.00

Page 7
CAPRICE amber water goblet – $125.00-150.00

Page 8
CAPRICE Moonlight Blue Doulton style pitcher – $4,000.00-4,500.00

Page 9
CAPRICE crystal pressed sherbet – $60.00-85.00
CHANTILLY crystal two part divided relish – $60.00-75.00

Page 10
CHANTILLY crystal Pristine divided bowl – $150.00-175.00
CHANTILLY crystal crescent salad plate – $85.00-100.00

Page 11
CLEO amber vase – $100.00-125.00

Page 12
CLEO Willow Blue candleholder – $100.00-125.00

Page 13
CLEO green tumbler – $65.00-75 .00

Page 14
DIANE crystal ruffled bowl – $75.00-85.00
DIANE iridized 3 part relish and celery – $75.00-100.00

Page 15
DIANE Emerald Green sea food cocktail – $75.00-100.00

Page 16
DIANE crystal footed oil – $110.00-135.00

Page 17
DIANE crystal tumbler – $30.00-35.00; decanter – $175.00-200.00

Page 18
ELAINE crystal top hat vase – $225.00-275.00

Page 19
ELAINE crystal 4 toed oval ram's head bowl – $150.00-200.00

Page 20
GLORIA amber pinch tumbler – $35.00-45.00;
pinch decanter – $250.00-300.00

Page 21
GLORIA Ebony with silver decoration candleholder – $40.00-50.00
GLORIA Ebony with silver decoration 4 toed bowl – $75.00-85.00

Page 22
GLORIA Heatherbloom cordial – $300.00-325.00

Page 23
GLORIA Gold Krystol tumbler – $35.00-45.00; decanter – $ 175.00-200.00

Page 24
IMPERIAL HUNT SCENE amber covered jug – $225.00-250.00

Page 25
PORTIA amber handled decanter – $300.00-350.00

Page 26
PORTIA after dinner cup and saucer – $100.00-125.00
PORTIA crystal ram's head candy box and cover – $150.00-175.00

Page 27
ROSALIE Bluebell water goblet – $75.00-85.00

Page 28
ROSALIE Topaz Aero Optic 8 oz. water – $50.00-60.00

Page 29
ROSALIE Willow Blue 2 oz. tumbler – $50.00-60.00
ROSEPOINT amber 5 compartment celery
and relish – $200.00-250.00

Page 30
ROSEPOINT crystal Pristine 18" pan bowl – $500.00-600.00;
ROSEPOINT crystal sugar – $100.00-125.00;
creamer – $115.00-140.00

Page 31
ROSEPOINT crystal 4 toed bonbon – $85.00-100.00

Page 32
ROSEPOINT crystal Pristine (Leaf) candlestick – $100.00-125.00

Page 33
ROSEPOINT crystal Pristine 6 part relish – $125.00-150.00

Page 34
ROSEPOINT crystal Pristine vase – $175.00-200.00

Page 35
ROSEPOINT Ebony, gold encrusted, 3 footed candy – $350.00-450.00

Page 36
ROSEPOINT Ebony, gold encrusted vase – $450.00-500.00

Page 37
SQUARE crystal tumbler with "crackle" effect – $40.00-50.00
SQUARE crystal ruffled top vase – $50.00-60.00

Page 38
WILDFLOWER Emerald 12" vase – $100.00-125.00

Page 39
WILDFLOWER amber, gold encrusted plate – $100.00-125.00

Page 40
CARIBBEAN blue opalescent 9" salad bowl – $125.00-150.00

Page 41
MADRID Golden Glo ash tray – $100.00-125.00

Page 42
GEORGIAN green lazy susan or cold cuts server – $700.00-800.00

Page 43
PARROT Golden Glo paperweight – $200.00+

Page 44
LINCOLN INN opalescent green sugar bowl – $75.00-100.00

Page 45
AMERICAN opaque blue hat – $150.00-200.00

Page 46
AMERICAN blue cologne bottle – $125.00-150.00

Page 47
AMERICAN crystal Tom & Jerry punch bowl – $600.00-750.00

Page 48
AMERICAN LADY amethyst cocktail – $60.00-75.00

Schroeder's
ANTIQUES Price Guide

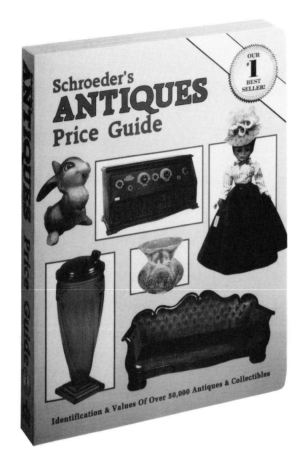

Schroeder's Antiques Price Guide is the #1 best-selling antiques & collectibles value guide on the market today, and here's why . . . More than 300 authors, well-known dealers, and top-notch collectors work together with our editors to bring you accurate information regarding pricing and identification. More than 45,000 items in almost 500 categories are listed along with hundreds of sharp original photos that illustrate not only the rare and unusual, but the common, popular collectibles as well. Each large close-up shot shows important details clearly. Every subject is represented with histories and background information, a feature not found in any of our competitors' publications. Our editors keep abreast of newly-developing trends, often adding several new categories a year as the need arises. If it merits the interest of today's collector, you'll find it in Schroeder's. And you can feel confident that the information we publish is up to date and accurate. Our advisors thoroughly check each category to spot inconsistencies, listings that may not be entirely reflective of market dealings, and lines too vague to be of merit. Only the best of the lot remains for publication. Without doubt, you'll find Schroeder's Antiques Price Guide the only one to buy for reliable information and values.

8½ x 11", 608 Pages   **$12.95**

COLLECTOR BOOKS
A Division of Schroeder Publishing Co., Inc.